Embodying the Wisdom of Immortality

I0142745

Embodying the Wisdom
of Immortality

Copyright ©2024 by Betsey Grobecker
betgrobecker@gmail.com

Cover design by Debbi Wraga

All rights reserved

ISBN Number: 978-1-60571-650-3

Printed in the United States of America

Embodying the Wisdom of Immortality

BETSEY GROBECKER

ONE

The Tiger

The tiger stands still,
  centered in its cage.
Its eyes, ablaze with the intensity of the sun, study
  every move of the *fearful* man locking its cage.
The man is seeking every speck of space
  between himself and the tiger.
He turns to walk away, and
  the tiger lurches from its cage.
"Is the cage an illusion?" I ask.

All is still.
Except for the throbbing pulse of
  my fear that fills space.
I hear no sounds from the tiger or the man,
  nor can I see them.
Yet, I know the tiger has eaten the man.

Another tiger and man fill my vision.
The tiger stands still,
  centered in its cage.
Its eyes, ablaze with the intensity of the sun, study
  every move of the *trustful* man locking his cage.

The man is excruciatingly close to the tiger's cage, and
   the tiger can easily swallow him up.

A dark cloud of doom hovers as
   I question if the man should trust the tiger.
The man turns to walk away,
   and my fear surges.
"He does not know the cage cannot hold the tiger, and
   the tiger has just eaten a man," I think.
But I cannot speak to him of the impending danger.

All is still.
Except for the throbbing pulse
   of my fear that fills space.
I hear no sounds from the tiger or the man,
   nor can I see them.
Yet, I know the tiger did *not* eat the man.

"The tiger knows who is enlightened,"
   I find myself saying as I awake from my dream.

I am enjoying dinner when
   the eyes of the tiger fill my inner vision.
Their radiating golden glow of inspiration touches me.
"Ah ha," I blurt out. "The tiger, the fearful man, and
   the trustful man are all acts
   of whom I can choose to be."

The golden inspirational glow of the tiger's eyes
   fills my inner Beingness.
"The faces you see are an illusion,
   just as my cage is an illusion.

Embodying the Wisdom of Immortality

They are creations of your rational mind
  whose imbalanced vision cannot perceive Light.
The remnants of your mind's fear and doubt
  pull you out of your center:
  the space of your spirited imagination.

It is time for wisdom to swallow up the residue
  of your fear and doubt.
And illumine the creative potential existing within,
  beyond all fear and doubt."

I surrender to the tiger's eyes.
Their vigorous radiance pulses within me,
  swallowing up the remnants of my fear and doubt.
Golden wisps of Light arise
  from within the depths of my Crystalline Heart.
They become wings of golden Light
  inviting me to fly.

I spread the wings of My spirited imagination, and
I fly through the bars of my illusionary cage of fear.
  My story begins . . .

Two

I am sitting in the circular sunroom of my parents' home that once held my father's telescope. My father had been a sought-after astronomer, but after about twenty years at a prestigious university, he accepted a job at a small teaching college. He said his passion took him outside the accepted boundaries of astronomy, and he wanted to create space to explore uncharted territory. The college was thrilled to have such a prestigious researcher among them and kept his workload uncommonly low. About fifteen years later, when my father retired, he donated his telescope to that college. When I asked why he gave away something he cherished, he said he wanted to give his attention to the expansion of his inner vision. Almost everything my parents shared about themselves, and their work made little sense to me, and I avoided getting into any detailed conversations with them, including my father's comment about expanding his inner vision.

My mother had once worked at the same renowned university, as an English professor, but shortly after they moved to western New York for my father's new job, she became pregnant with me. During her pregnancy, she tried publishing without a university affiliation and stayed an independent writer for the rest of her life. I was an only child. I had few memories of my early childhood, but I continued to vividly recall the love that filled the space of our home and how safe I once felt in that love. However, as I matured into my teen years, I became acutely aware of how different my parents were from my friends' parents. They were just not what I defined as normal, and I sometimes felt ashamed by their eccentric ways. They made efforts to show interest in things that were important to me, but I knew their hearts were elsewhere. So, I found space from them, and this space grew as I matured. Once I went away to college, I seldom visited or phoned them, and our distance grew as the years passed. They never pressured me to change my ways.

I was now well into my forties. Although married for a fleeting time years ago, I was divorced, without children or a partner. In my younger years, I dated on and off after my divorce and discovered that I did not want to commit to another marriage. My marriage had been difficult, and my beliefs about marriage were too shattered for me to repair. However, I put my biases aside when I was with my clients.

I was a psychiatrist, and I had invested endless energy building my private practice. It paid off, as it blossomed, providing me with a sense of importance in the eyes of others and in my own eyes. The respect of my peers, which I craved, diminished the humiliation associated with my parents. Lately, however, my years of demanding work have been catching up with me. I was tired, and my enthusiasm had waned. My work was no longer the "mend" to my need for fulfillment. Something was not right about my work, and I was becoming increasingly dissatisfied with what I had once cherished. I attributed my angst to a midlife crisis that would pass to minimize my growing misery.

Embodying the Wisdom of Immortality

The sun was stunningly bright today, so bright that even I noticed it. Its rays reflected on the vibrant colors of the Universe my father had painted on the sunroom floor where the telescope once stood years ago. To my great surprise, I sometimes sensed the artwork vibrating during those few occasions when I visited as if to call my attention to it. But I ignored these sensations, fearful that my parents' eccentricity was in my genes. I did not want to be like them, and I did everything I could to distance myself from their strange world. Now, however, my thoughts and feelings about my parents were haunting me. Two days ago, one of their friends called to tell me they had passed away in a boating accident on Lake Erie. They were in their mid-seventies and loved to sail. My parents were always careful, knowing their limits, but an unexpected storm with a heavy gale blew in, toppling their sailboat. Rescue came too late. I was in shock from their sudden death and despondent. My years of cold-heartedness toward them were in my face. In my desperation for consolation, I opened to receive the warm glow of the sun's rays streaming through the room and began to sob. The more I sobbed, the deeper my breath moved inside me, loosening my anguish while lifting me from the heaviness of my despair.

The library, where my parents had worked, was near the sunroom at the back of the house. I refused to enter its space for years, but a deep curiosity to know the secrets the room held awakened within me. I hesitantly entered. My father had covered its dome ceiling with his artwork of the night sky when I was young. And, for the first time since I was young, its radiating brilliance touched me with its beauty. "How could I have negated his stunning artwork?" I asked myself.

Lightheaded and dizzy, I found the nearest chair to sit on. Closing my eyes, I saw myself as a child. My parents and I were taking turns looking through the telescope, into the night sky. The constellations and planets shimmered with aliveness to my young eyes, and a faint memory of their pulsing rhythm breathing through me returned. Now I wondered if those sensations were real or mere fantasies of my childhood mind.

Looking around the library, I saw pictures I had painted as a child on the wall. A couple of them were of black holes with my mother's poems next to them. Black holes fascinated my parents, and my mother often wrote poetry and short stories about them. My parents said black holes were of the mysterious, infinite depths within the sacred Heart of every single living form on Earth. Their radiant depths illuminated all creation, even the sun and me. I must have shared their fascination with black holes because I painted a lot of them. Deciding to take a closer look at my work, I stood, checked my balance, and slowly approached my favorite painting with my mother's poem next to it.

Ellen's Black Hole

Ellen is of the Great Mystery:
  the mysterious Love of the radiant darkness
  deep within the depths of her sacred Heart.
Its sublime essence imagines all creation into being.

The radiant darkness of Ellen's Heart pulses
  with the songs of Its creative imagination.
Opening to receive the splendor of her Heart's beauty,
  Ellen breathes Its rhythmic songs into her creation.
And, as Ellen releases the beauty of her creation
  into the Universe,
Her breath flows back into her Heart
  to breathe songs of ever greater beauty
  into her creations.

Ellen is the Love, Brilliance, and Innocence
   of Great Mystery.
She is the magician, forever reimagining life.
Ellen knows no birth. Ellen knows no death.
She knows only the cycle of
   her Heart's ever-expanding beauty.

In my painting, my seven-year-old body was empty inside, except for my heart. A luminous black paint filled the space within my body as well as a stream of golden musical notes that flowed out from my heart and around the many stars I had drawn in the night sky. A couple of stars were falling from the sky and moving toward my heart. I reread the poem at least five times, each time taking a closer look at my painting, which I could barely believe I drew. And as I did so, the sensations of the words touched me more deeply. The part of me that wanted to dismiss what I was feeling as complete gibberish showed itself loud and clear, but I could no longer do so. I sighed and decided to move on and take care of the pressing needs of my parents' cremation. In their will, they asked that I release their ashes over Lake Erie, into its open space.

I ordered dinner and was soon in the bedroom of my childhood home. For the entirety of my adult years, I had known only discomfort in this space, but tonight, it felt like a protective cave embracing all my troubles and worries. I put my head on my pillow, gave my worries to the embrace of the protective cave of my childhood room, and fell into a sound sleep.

Angie was at my door soon after I showered and ate breakfast. She had been a close friend of my parents for years, even though she was at least twenty years younger than them. I knew she had her own business as a massage therapist but little more. She was a close friend of my parents, and her friendship with them was enough for me to brush her off; she was weird by association. It was Angie who relayed the news of my parents' passing to me. At that time, she offered her help with the necessary arrangements, which I gratefully accepted.

"How are you feeling?" Angie asked in a tone that held compassion, but which lacked the heaviness of grief. Even her black Italian eyes radiated lightness. Unused to a presence of lightness after the sudden death of a close friend, I became suspicious about what agendas she may be hiding, and I questioned if I could trust her. She sensed my hesitation.

"Ken and Rose left their bodies doing what they had always loved. While on Earth, they lived within a space that was of beauty and creativity. And I know they continue to live within that expanded space, even without their bodies. I'll miss their physical presence, but I continue to feel their spirits. Their inner beauty is, and always has been, the essence of our shared relationship. Recently, they said their bodies were tired, and perhaps it was time to offer them to the earth. I wasn't surprised about their passing."

A week ago, I would have dismissed a person who spoke such nonsense, but Angie's eyes touched my heart, just as my mother's poem and my painting touched me, and I sensed the truth in her words. My mother was of Asian descent, and although Angie's black eyes had a different shape, I recalled the same Light dancing in my mother's eyes when I was a kid. And as a kid, I trusted both of my parents' eyes. My father's eyes were auburn, like my eyes, and my mother said she married him because of his tiger eyes. I loved my father's eyes, too, as a kid and vaguely recalled how he would sometimes become the shape of a tiger through my childhood eyes. "Was that vision real?" I pondered. Anxiety began to overwhelm me as I felt my solid reality cracking. My mind was a ball of yarn, dropped from my confused, shaky hands. I did not know when it would stop unraveling and if I could put the ball back together again. I didn't even know if I wanted the ball back together as it was before.

My dizziness returned. I sat at the kitchen table and asked Angie if she would get me a glass of water. After doing so, she sat across from me in silence. On occasion, her eyes met mine as if to assure me that all was fine. I heard her breath and found myself breathing in rhythm to her breath. Slowly, my anxiety subsided. It was strange how her silence relaxed me, as I did not like silence and always kept it to a minimum. If I were not talking aloud, I would fill my silence with my ceaseless thoughts.

In time, I finished my water, and we began talking about plans for my parents. The storm had left my parents' boat beyond repair, but Angie knew a person who regularly sailed his own boat, adding that he knew my parents well. She would contact him to make the arrangements if I wanted her to. Two days later, Angie, and what I could feel of my childhood innocence were on the sailboat. Accompanying us were two urns holding my parents' ashes. Somewhere deep down, within the innocence of my childhood heart that I once existed within, I sensed my parents' spirits with us as well.

It was a perfect sailing day. Billowing white clouds cooled the heating sun of spring, and the wind, free of its fury, guided the sails onward. When we were far out onto the lake, I blindly reached for an urn and saw I had picked up my father's ashes. Inviting the wind to take them where they needed to go, I opened the urn, and the wind lifted them high into the sky. The clouds that had covered the sun suddenly blew away, unveiling the golden eyes of a tiger within the sun's glowing body. I instantly recognized them as my father's eyes, ablaze in a Light that had always touched my childhood eyes with their secrets.

"How eloquently you released my ashes to the wind. As an adult, you saw only my body, but as a child you also saw, and felt, my soul that had enjoyed its creative ventures with your soul. Your spirited imagination, which knows no limits, is always present deep within the uncluttered space of your Beingness. But your breath has become shallow and impure with the energy of your unbending beliefs and judgments. Open your heart to receive the loving wisdom deep within the core of your Beingness and allow your spirit's Light to burn what must go. You have the courage and the strength to understand your mind's fear-based limitations and to transcend them."

The wind swirled about me playfully, lifting the weight of my seriousness. I closed my eyes, inviting its playful swirls to blow away the hardened energies of the person I had become. Angie was staring out at the lake. The wind lifted her long black hair into it, and her hair became my mother's long black hair dancing with the wind. When Angie turned to face me, it was my mother's face. "Never question magic," I sensed my mother's eyes saying, then her eyes looked out at the lake again.

I immediately took my mother's urn in my hands. Breathing the swirling wind about me into my breath, I opened its lid. The wind slowed as I released her ashes to it while guiding them to the water with gentleness and ease. The ashes caressed the top of the lake as the wind that held them danced in synchrony with the lake's flow. Quite suddenly, and for only a moment, all became breathtakingly still. Everything disappeared from my awareness except for the unusually slow, graceful flow of the ashes onto the lake's mirror-like surface. The majesty that filled the moment suspended all time and its motion.

Feeling as if I had just awakened from a dream state, the wind once again flowed about me, and ripples returned to the lake's surface. A small whirlpool appeared, swallowing up my mother's ashes within its mysterious darkness. From within the center of the whirlpool, my mother's dark eyes appeared, and the sun's golden rays, reflecting upon them, danced like fireflies throughout their darkness. The playful dance of Light within her dark eyes mesmerized me, and I felt its joy. "The magic of your spirited imagination is fully alive within the radiant darkness of your inner depths. Is it not time to burn what does not serve your spirit's Light and unveil Its beauty within? My poetry is a metaphor for life's deep mysteries, and you will know and absorb Its secrets only when you 'hear' it from within the space of your inner Heart." My mother's eyes disappeared into the lake, and I no longer saw any trace of them. But I knew they had spoken to me, inviting me into the reality she had known on Earth and that she continued to know.

All remained silent as we sailed back, except for the wind that carried the boat home. Amazingly, the joyful songs of the wind caught my attention rather than the familiar drone of my thoughts. For the first time in a long, long time, I felt peace.

THREE

A week passed since I released my parents' ashes into the lake, and I had not seen anyone since then. Angie called every day to check on me, and today, we talked briefly about a gathering to celebrate my parents' life. She knew the people who would like to be part of that celebration and offered to make the arrangements for them to come to her home. She suggested a date that was about two weeks away. While I offered my help, halfheartedly, I also told her I trusted her judgment with the arrangements. I had always reviewed every detail of an event related to my work with my office manager, Jean, and did not readily give up control. But I was too exhausted and overwhelmed with life to even consider giving my attention to details, and I really did trust Angie. There was something quite beautiful about her black eyes that filled her oval face. I wasn't sure how her sturdy, tall body could express the gentleness that I sensed through her entire being, and I wondered why I had never noticed the lightness of her presence before. I also questioned how it was possible for me to be so blind to the beauty that I was beginning to sense in my parents' work and the magic I was beginning to recall as a kid.

Most days, I went to Lake Erie's harbor to feel the wind that caressed the lake's surface and filled the sails of boats with their strength. "Without the wind, there would be no movement," I thought. Increasingly, I opened my heart to feel the sensations of the wind playfully touching my body. The wind carried my father's ashes to the sun and my mother's ashes over the water before stilling itself to release her ashes into it. My father's ashes, now blended with the wind, would someday fill the clouds and flow back into Earth's body as water, just as my mother's ashes, now blended with the water, would flow into the heavens to form clouds, only to return into Earth's body as water. Angie was right. My parents were far from dead. There was an essence, something far greater than their mind and body that lived on, and I even sensed their presence at times.

My staunch beliefs about the human psyche, as I understood it, were loosening. Mainstream psychiatry did not accept anything beyond the chemical physiology of the human mind and body, and the related emotional/environmental experiences of a person, to explain the human psyche. Carl Jung, however, spoke of archetypes: the inherited collective and structural elements of our primitive psyche. He believed our rational mind has lost its connection to these deeper, instinctive forces that make us whole. We need to confront unhealthy, personal energies and dissolve them to expand into the pure, potent energies of our instinctive psyche. While I did not understand the nature and source of the essence I experienced on the lake, I sensed it was something unique from an inherited energy.

I recognized the signs of experiencing a "crack" in the reality that held things in place, and I knew exactly what I needed to do to "glue" my cracking Humpty Dumpty shell back together again. Yet, I did not want to go down that path after my experience on the lake. I had to face my fear of the unknown and allow my shell to crack wide open, even though I was risking my reputation as the epitome of a levelheaded, esteemed psychiatrist to do so. The beliefs of my old monarch had to fall, and my guides were my parents' books and artwork in the library. I believed that if I gave myself time and space, I would find my way through this change while still taking care of my needs. I was beginning to understand why my parents left their prestigious university positions and made the choices that followed.

I called Jean, who mirrored the highly proficient and organized person I had once known myself to be. Everything was black and white, lacking the most minute traces of gray. She never negated any details related to her responsibilities, and she had efficiently connected my clients to other psychiatrists for what I initially believed would be a three-month leave. But three months was not enough time now, and I told Jean I needed a year to take care of things and wanted to close the office during that time. Knowing she would need to look for another job, I offered her six months of severance pay. Her competency in running a psychiatric office was well known, and six months was more time than she needed to find work. However, I wanted to acknowledge her years of work, and my savings and inheritance enabled me to be generous. Although surprised by my announcement, I heard no anxiety in Jean's voice. She, too, knew that work would readily find its way to her. I knew she welcomed the paid time off. She would take care of the details to close the office for a year and did not need my help to do so.

I poured myself some iced lemon water. I felt relief to have time for myself, but I was not free of anxiety for what was ahead. I took my water into the sunroom to enjoy the beauty of the spring day. Flowers were beginning to bloom, and for a few seconds, I could swear I heard them hum through the open windows as they swayed about in the gentle breeze. "What am I getting myself into?" I asked aloud, then affirmed my commitment to delve deeper into my parents' work and my own inner psyche.

The coolness of the liquid refreshed me, and I increasingly relaxed my mind and body. It was odd how the room felt so much lighter today. My eyes fell upon the pale, blue-green painting of Neptune on the floor of the sunroom, and I went into the library to see if I could find any poems about it. My mother authored the poetry, but my father's insights about astronomy guided the content of much of it. On occasion, my father's artwork went with the poetry, but he kept his name anonymous. I saw shelves labeled with each planet's name, randomly selected a book under "Neptune," then returned to the sunroom. Opening the book to a random page, I read the poem on it.

Neptune: The Mysterious Radiance Beyond Creation

I AM the eternal essence of Spirit's life force
  permeated in all-pervasive Love.
I AM spaceless space,
  free of time: boundless and limitless.
I AM Pure Consciousness,
  empty of creation's energies,
  yet mysteriously illumined with the vibratory ripple
  that set all creation in motion.
I AM the entirety of the yet-to-be-birthed
  electromagnetic field of Consciousness.

My creative passion burns with desire
  to bring forth in My own Image.
My unbounded space gathers Itself into a point:
  the Heart of the Universe.
My primal wind swirls about, filling the Heart
  with the Light of the first creative principle:

the Original Intellect that is the Original One.

You Are of the Pure Consciousness that envelopes you.
Fall into My blanket of all-pervasive Love.
   BE of My Awareness.

I put the book down and breathed, my eyes focused on the painting of Neptune. Suddenly, its form expanded, taking on depth, and I became aware of liquids swirling about with immense passion deep within its body. It was an intensely stormy sea, far beyond the expansiveness of anything I had ever known, and its potency was magnifying beyond what I could take in. I looked away so that the storm would not shred me into pieces. Dizzy, I took deep breaths to ground myself back into my body, but it was difficult to do so. "Was my own psyche whirling, or was the painting of Neptune whirling, or were we both whirling? Am I an electromagnetic field of Consciousness?" I asked my exceedingly confused self.

I heard Angie's voice and tried to open my eyes, but they were so heavy, I could open them just enough to get a glimpse of her. Her muscular body was vibrating with immense aliveness, making it appear far less solid, and her voice touched me as my parents' voice had touched me on the lake. I was not even sure if the words were coming from her mouth. "Did I die or land on an alien planet?" I tried to communicate, bewildered.

"Ellen, there is nothing for you to fear," Angie communicated to me, even though I was unsure exactly how. I could see my body, but my awareness was outside of my body, and I knew only pure bliss. Angie's words flowed from her mouth as waves of Light that somehow spoke to me beyond my physical ears. "You didn't answer the phone this morning, so I came to check on you. I see the book on your lap, and I know what is happening. Your parents' work vibrates with the purity of potent, refined Light, far more dynamic than what your biology can resonate with right now. Sensing the beauty of this presence, you opened your heart to receive it. It entered your body like a bolt of lightning, and your biology was unable to manage the intensity and purity of this Light. Right now, you are aware outside of your body, within a dimension of spacetime that this Light can sing in harmony with. While a connection to your mind and body is still present, they are in shock right now as they try to adapt to the intensity and purity of this energy.

"The good news is that the force of physical gravity, which bonded your thoughts together in their addictive, hardened patterns within your biology, has loosened. Your mind will be far less resistant to integrating the Light you now know. However, it is an extremely fragile time as your biology tries to regain its balance and stabilize itself in the Light within which you are now aware. I do not know how long this process will take, and you will continue to feel disoriented and not fully present as your biology adjusts. I will help you through this process."

Angie brought a straw to my mouth. "It's important that you drink this, Ellen. It will help you. You want to keep the small connection you still have with your mind and body. Slowly, this connection will grow."

Sensing the importance of Angie's words, I made the effort to do as asked, but with difficulty. The liquid's warmth was soothing, and my bewildered body did what it could to allow its comforting sensations to seep into it. When she removed the straw, I withdrew my focus from my body. A brilliant Light was before me that assumed the shape of a tiger. Its auburn eyes were the eyes of my father, and their Light spoke directly to the Light that I was experiencing.

"How brave and adventurous you are to delve within, to realize the mystery of your unspeakably pure, translucent, inner Beingness. You, I, and every single life form, whether miniscule or gigantic or present with or without a body, are beings of radiating, pulsing Light. Although I am no longer present within my physical body, I am present *as* the Awareness of my Lightbody. I am communicating directly to your sacred Heart through the Light that my Awareness is emitting. At the same time, my Lightbody is drawing into It and receiving all that It needs to support Its creative evolution. The positive, emitting life force of my spirit and the negative, receiving life force of my Heart dance in harmony with each other. Unified within the Love of my crystalline center, they charge and recharge my electrified field, forever sustaining and evolving the spiraling flow of my breath: the vital force of my Lightbody.

"All life radiates gravity, but most humans, even scientists, are unaware of nonphysical gravity: the Light of our spirit that lifts energy. Physical gravity bonds energy together to solidify our awareness into mental and physical forms. Without the consolidating powers of this gravity, we would not have our physical bodies, nor could we focus our senses to give form to what had been formless. However, for quite some time, the polarized charges of male and female energies have been vibrating at different frequencies within our DNA. Their imbalanced frequencies create friction, and this friction has pulled our awareness from our Heart center; it is no longer able to flow within the multidimensional layers of our inner Beingness. Flowing only within the dense, linear Earth realm of our Beingness, the suctioning power of physical gravity has bonded the energy of our thoughts into shallow, repetitive patterns of action and reaction. When we allow the nonphysical gravity of spirit's Light to pierce our minds and drink Its purity into us, Its Light loosens the force of our thoughts while transmuting their impurities. Space opens within us, and Light illuminates what was once darkness.

"A New Energy, a Light whose polarized charges vibrate at the same frequency suitable to them, is beginning to radiate Its presence on Earth, and this is the Light you have opened to receive. Its crystalline purity is without the push/pull dynamics of duality, which have occupied our biology for so long. Its purity has offset your entire biology; it does not know where its center of stability is. Your new center will be your crystalline Heart, not your mind and ego. It will take some time for your mind and body to accept this highly subtle energy and come into balance within your inner Heart. But in time, all energy will flow outward from your pure, crystalline Heart and return to It.

"Angie has broken through the fortress of her mind's conditioned thought patterns of action and reaction and embraced the crystalline energies within the open space of her core. She has shed the difference between the positive, emitting life force of her spirit, and the negative, receiving Love of her inner Heart, and her purified biology now spins within the unity energy of multidimensionality. Fully present within the mystical Love of her inner Heart, her breath flows inward, into her timeless depths, to touch the Light of her spirit's imagination and outward, into time, to give form to Its inspiration. Trust her and trust the Light and Love of the Awareness into which you are awakening. Know that fear is an illusion of your mind and breathe through the Love and Light of the cosmic wind. Nurture your mind and body with acceptance and love for all that has been. Breathe through Love, not fear."

As my father's eyes faded, I became aware of Angie moving my body onto my bed from a wheelchair while saying something about someone dropping the chair off for me. Although I was extremely disoriented, I knew no fear. The expansiveness of the Light I now knew was beyond any beauty that I could have ever imagined. My only desire was to expand deeper within this Light, whatever the cost to do so.

FOUR

D aily routines slowly found their way into my life. While I continued to have little balance and strength, and my mind lacked focus, I did what I could to help Angie. She lived nearby and visited three times each day. Her morning and afternoon visits were short, but she stayed at least an hour every night to recite one of my mother's poems, or to give me a massage. Her visit last night was brief as it was the night that people were gathering to celebrate my parents' life. Today, Angie shared details about the celebration. Even though she kept them simple, I understood only bits and pieces of the event. However, I did sense the joy present in the celebration. She had shared my situation with two of my parents' closest friends, Eliza, and Daniel, and they offered their help if I was comfortable with the idea. Angie said Daniel had sailed my parents' boat the day I released their ashes into the lake, but I barely noticed him. Glad that Angie had their help, my heavy head slowly nodded my approval.

Eliza was a retired opera singer. She was in her early fifties, but she could not use her voice as she once did when she was young without straining it. Short, wavy flames of red hair surrounded her deep blue eyes that filled her round face. She exuded a vibrant aliveness, and there were times when I could swear her hair was alive with flames of light that made its waves dance as they stretched into the skies. Creative passion beamed from within her depthless, sky-blue eyes and sang through the vibrant robustness of her voice, and this passionate Love assured me that all was well. I knew that Eliza, too, breathed the loving Light of her inner depths through her Beingness.

One day, Eliza shared her story of how my parents changed her life. As with Angie, her words communicated to me beyond my ears, and as she spoke, an image of a younger Eliza appeared. She was reciting a poem, written by my mother, while breathing into the Light that flowed from it. "Are my mother's words Light steeped into the print?" I wondered.

When finished, Eliza put the book down, closed her eyes, then breathed deeply for a while. As Light danced around and into her deepening breath, the tension about her heart loosened, and her breath expanded into the space opening within her heart. Then she stood tall and began singing the scales. Pulsing waves of profoundly clear, colorless Light began to seep into her heart. Her physical body almost disappeared to this pulsing flow of Light through every space it could find as she sang. Eliza slowly released control of her breath to this sacredness, just as I was releasing my own breath to this unspeakable majesty. While the Light flowing through her was a shallow stream, I knew I was a witness to the beginning of her inner transformation, just as she was a witness to my own change. I now understood the profound beauty resonating through her singing.

As my vision disappeared, I heard Eliza's slow, carefully enunciated speech that she used when talking to me. "The work of Ken and Rose spoke to a space deep inside me, and when my husband and I moved here a couple of years ago after retiring, we became good friends. We were fortunate to retire young, as we both had interests outside of our former work that we wanted to give our attention to. I accept an offer to perform

Embodying the Wisdom of Immortality

an opera now and then, but I am free of my heavy travel schedule and related pressures, and I do not need to use my voice to reach those extremely high opera notes as often as I once did. I love singing, just to sing, and singing to you gives me immense pleasure. I often sing songs that have little to do with opera now, and I'm really enjoying exploring other music genres that do not strain my voice as opera does."

Eliza put my lunch of soft, solid foods, which I was now eating, on the table while handing me a spoon. I continued to miss many details of conversations, but I was getting the gist of their words, and I tried to respond. "Beautiful story, Eliza. Your singing is magic that uplifts me," I managed to say as I clumsily maneuvered my spoon to get food into my mouth. Light beamed through her smiling eyes, and I opened to receive the fullness of It.

Eliza left me sitting in the sunroom, and I was looking at my father's artwork covering its floor. Pluto was calling my attention to it, and I vaguely recalled a conversation with my father about Pluto.

"Why did you include Pluto in your painting when you know it's recognized only as a dwarf planet?" In my black and white world, devoid of grays, the objectivity of science ruled. I never breached its sacred boundaries.

My father's eyes appeared to smile at me, and I quickly rejected the possibility that eyes could smile. "Scientists continue to debate its status as a planet. However, it was my intuition that guided me to include it in my painting, and I listen to my inner sense above the beliefs of others. The essence that Pluto stands for makes it necessary to include it in the Universe."

He stopped and looked at me, as if to ask permission to continue, and I did not give it. Instead, I sighed and walked away. "What planet are my parents on? Why can't I figure out what is wrong with them

-27-

that makes them so weird?" Even my trusted *Diagnostic and Statistical Manual of Mental Disorders,* used to categorize mental and emotional difficulties, did not provide answers.

The blindness of my eyes at that time was painful, and I was grateful Angie walked in as I began to fall into the rabbit hole of my anguish. I shared, as best I could, what just happened.

Angie laughed, helping me to laugh at my monstrous guilt and shame for who I once was and my disrespectful attitude toward my parents. "You're a psychiatrist, and I'm aware that you have your own interpretation for why your shadow is showing itself to you. I see things quite differently, and if you want to hear my point of view, I'm happy to share it with you."

I nodded.

"Your awareness has opened to the intuitive wisdom of your inner depths. As your biology begins to adjust to this subtle presence, the Love within your mystical Heart is 'shedding Light' on the shadows that were hiding in the darkness. Your guilt and shame are rooted within your biology as living parasites that feed off your cells while planting their toxicity within them. The imbalanced energies of your shadow are surfacing to find resolution and dissolve. However, your mind must allow the loving Light of your expanding awareness to transmute these toxins into the nectar of Love. Love, only, can resolve the powerful force of your biology's deeply rooted shadow energies and illuminate your Truth, beyond the veil of shadow energies. Allow your divinity to burn the impurities of your shadow into unrecognizable ashes whose purified essence will reintegrate into your crystalline core."

Angie's words pierced the space opening within me that didn't require my mind to understand them. It was odd how I had a difficult time following the ordered events of this world, but at the same time, I was becoming increasingly aware of an intuitive sense that gleaned what Light was sharing. Through the expanded awareness that my cracked psyche had jolted me into, I *felt* the unspeakable brilliance and clarity of Light's presence. My mind, however, had not yet integrated with this Light. So, while it could repeat words, it questioned Light's subtle presence simply because its logic could not yet be in balance with the grace It held.

As part of my psychiatric training, I had explored my own inner depths through mental analysis and was aware of my parental influences and related conflicts. However, I assumed I had resolved my issues, and they no longer affected me. Although I could not diagnose my parents' behaviors, I believed them to be beyond the range of what is normal. So, I need not carry guilt for the distance I kept from them. But now I was beginning to reap the understanding that my parents' "abnormality" was their transcendence from the shared human consciousness within which I had existed.

I was also coming to understand that I could not resolve the powerful life force of my mind's shadow energies by using the powers of my mind. Attempting to do so would only hinder the efforts for my mind to accept an essence that did not feed off its life force. The Light I felt was far more dynamic and complete than what my mind could ever know through its own powers alone. How I once understood the nature of the psyche and how to work with it were changing dramatically. In fact, to accept the notion that we are a Lightbody, a flow of conscious Awareness within the multidimensional layers of our crystalline core, was not even within the realm of possibility not so long ago. How very deluded I was!

Recently, Angie began to play her favorite songs, including a handful of Eliza's songs, before reciting one of my mother's poems or while giving me a massage. Today, when she put one of Eliza's CDs in the stereo, I closed my eyes, and the dark radiance of the night sky filled the space within them. Everything in the sky, even the glowing darkness of space itself, pulsed with balanced aliveness. As my breath slowly blended with the rhythm of this pulse, my mind was able to release the tightness of its guilt into the free-flowing currents of the space opening within it. The brilliance of my father's smiling, tiger eyes briefly filled two frozen craters of the distant planet, Pluto, then his eyes came together as one eye. Everything disappeared from this eye, except for its dark pupil, which began to swirl at an immense speed while filling with Light.

"Don't be deceived by the limitations of what the human mind and its tools perceive," the wind of the eye roared through me. "Pluto is radiantly alive as the Consciousness of the Original Intellect: the wholeness of the brilliant, electromagnetic field of radiating Awareness from which all has originated and to which all will return. Every single biological form, including your own body, has its origin within this Original Intellect, while at the same time, each unique being stays centered within this Original Intellect. Far beyond your physical mind and body, deep within your spacious, radiant depths, the brilliance of the Original Intellect pulses. Empty yourself of your conditioned human self. Release what does not serve your deepest Truth. Unveil the spacious, radiant depths of your exquisite wholeness."

The winds of swirling Light dissipated into the radiant darkness of the dark pupil as my vision disappeared. I heard Eliza's singing on the CD, and the crystalline clarity of her voice pulsed with mystical Love. As this Love covered me, it helped to dissolve my mind's doubt of Its reality. Angie's breath synchronized with this Love, inviting my body to breathe through it, but my biology was unable to take in its fullness. "Patience and ongoing trust and attunement to the presence of a life force far greater than your mind are all you need to focus on now," I sensed Angie communicating to me. Everything was shifting in my reality, including how I understood the words that others spoke to me.

I had no idea how much time had passed when I heard Angie put a glass of iced tea next to me. I slowly opened my eyes and grinned at her body of Light before me.

"Interested in a poem about Pluto?"

Angie knew how much I loved my mother's poetry, and I never turned down the opportunity for her to recite me a poem. I nodded with excitement.

Pluto: The Universal Heart of the Original Intellect

I AM awakened, sublime Love:
  the original pulsing Heart of the Creative Universe.
I AM aware *as* the electromagnetic field of Consciousness
  ablaze with passion
  to evolve the unborn Universe of my Beingness.
I AM the center point:
The Universal Heart
  from which all life originates,
  and to which all life returns.

My passion burns to create in My image.
My One becomes two:
  primal Spirit and primal Heart.
Each elemental force is with its own unique Heart center
  while simultaneously unified with My Universal Heart.

You are the Original Intellect
  centered within the Original Intellect, and
The Original Intellect is You
  centered within You.

Within the depths of your very own psyche,
the Universal Heart pulses with utmost purity and brilliance.
Realize your Immortality.

As Angie recited the poem, I lost all attention to her words. My arms became feathers of golden Light that lifted me to dance. I stretched my wings high into the heavens, then deep into the roots of Earth's body, and returned my wings back into the heavens, repeatedly. My entire being became a circle of spiraling feathers of Light—counterclockwise and clockwise, inward and outward—about my still, radiating center of Love. Surrendering to the immense purity of this mystical Love, my separate movements joined together as a stream of free-flowing, vibrant Light through the unified centers of my Heart and the Universal Heart. My only desire was to keep expanding into the immense beauty I had become.

The songs of the birds woke me as the sun's early rays stretched themselves beyond Earth's horizon and into the space of the sunroom. I fell asleep in the chair I sat in last night and could not remember Angie finishing the poem. The sweetness of the birds' songs enticed me to get up and dance, but as I tried to lift myself, I remembered I had a physical body that was going through a deep transformation. I was uncharacteristically patient with the time needed for my biology to adjust and be strong again. I could never return to the person I once was and the energies that fed and sustained the beliefs I held. I carefully maneuvered my body from my chair and into my wheelchair, then gave myself a sponge bath. By the time Angie arrived, I had already dressed myself.

Angie was all smiles. The fact that I was able to bathe and dress myself for the first time must have planted those smiles in her eyes. While making breakfast, she suggested it may be time for me to begin transitioning to a walker. "Some of my clients have problems with their strength and balance, and I know where to get a walker specifically designed for people like yourself. Getting your body into an upright position and walking would help to advance your progress at this point."

"My body is getting stronger, and my balance is improving, although slowly. I want to try the walker."

"Let me give this transition some more thought before we go ahead with this. Daniel's coming today, right?"

I nodded.

"I'd appreciate his opinion, and I'll give him a call to see if he's willing to assess your strength and balance, if that's OK with you."

Again, I nodded my agreement.

I liked Daniel, just as I liked Angie and Eliza, although he was quite different from them. His parents raised him in the rural outskirts of western New York. His father fished for a living, and they grew much of their own food to make ends meet. He had immensely disliked school and did as little as he could to get through. When he was in tenth grade, his father took him, and his younger brother out on a sailboat. As he lost himself to the majesty of the wind, he discovered his great love for sailing.

The first day Daniel came to visit, his turquoise eyes, threaded with the sun's golden rays that extended deep into their depths, captivated me. He was not much younger than me. His weather-worn, sailor skin dressed his muscular body, and his skin glowed with the softness of a morning sun that had not yet bloomed into the completeness of its majesty. Daniel was not a big talker, seeming to prefer silence. Although he offered no reasons for his quiet nature, I sensed he wanted to hear only the pulse of the cosmic winds that flowed through the vastness of space within and without him. Even on the hottest summer days, he preferred the windows open.

I was surprised by my enjoyment of Daniel's silence. I suppose I could now appreciate his serenity. It was his intuition of how the wind moved, within and without his Beingness, and how to sustain his balance through the worst of storms, which helped me find my own sense of balance and my confidence in it as we tested my gait. If I gave my full attention to each step, I could manage with his support. He said if I used the walker only when someone was with me, he would tell Angie to pick one up, and I concurred with this arrangement. A few weeks later, Daniel donated my wheelchair to charity.

He had put a ramp over the few steps of the back entrance, and a chair, easy to get in and out of, kept the ramp and myself company. Most days, I sat outside after breakfast. Angie began calling in the morning, rather than coming over. As time passed and my strength and balance grew, I told Eliza and Daniel that I could manage without their help. However, once a week they still stopped by at lunchtime to check in on me, and I always enjoyed their visits.

When I told Angie it was not necessary for her to come every night, she shared how much she was enjoying her nightly visits. "Although I've read every one of your mother's poems, the secrets they hold are depthless. The more I open my heart to receive the Love and wisdom they hold; the more grace guides my day. You're still in a fragile, vulnerable time as your mind and body continue to adjust to and integrate the expanded Awareness of who you are becoming, and I want to continue my visits. Let's see how things go, and I'll let you know when I feel more comfortable cutting back on my nightly visits."

I nodded my agreement.

FIVE

M y routines continued, for how long I do not know, as I had lost all track of time. Time itself felt confining, beyond my willingness to contain myself within, and I noted the passing of summer by the beauty the leaves were now sharing. My time-oriented, structured life of black and white, devoid of any grays, was dissolving into the balanced winds of wisdom where gray was the harmonic dance between what were once tension-filled polarities. I was surrendering who I had known myself to be as the astute, boundary-adhering psychiatrist of rational science, to the intuitive, loving Light within my parents' home and my expanding house of Light within. The shadow parts of me continued to arise. However, my house of Light, within and without, made it easier for me to embrace their hardened force as I breathed the expanded, loving presence of my own soul and spirit through my Beingness.

While I was still gaining a sense of orientation, the force of my mind was diminishing. It was slowly trusting the intuitive presence of my soul and learning how to work in harmony with the expansive Light that I had unwittingly opened to receive. I was in undefined territory: the Ellen who I had been was fading as the future Ellen was gestating. My space of existence was within the timeless, nonphysical water of my inner, creative womb, which was imagining into being what was yet to be born. If I chose to let go of the Light to return to the known comfort zone of my mind's ways, my golden wings would not be set free to fly. I had to stay with the process of trusting the Light as the former me slowly surrendered to Its creative vision.

When Daniel surprised me with a visit today, I began sharing some of what I was experiencing. But I did not get far because the golden threads within his sky-blue eyes began to pulse inward and outward, just as the tides and currents of the ocean flowed. "Ride the tides and currents of the open ocean with me," his eyes beckoned. Accepting their invitation, I lost myself to his pulsing eyes that took me far out onto the ocean. We were on a golden sailboat with sails of translucent wings that floated our boat above the water's surface.

"Surrender your breath, Ellen, to the magnificence of the wind that pulses throughout the luminous wings of our boat." And as I opened the entirety of my Beingness to welcome the flow of the awe-inspiring wind within me, the golden threads that had filled Daniel's eyes became waves of Light that his physical body dissipated into, and his Lightbody flowed within a larger field of pulsing Light that had once been the ocean. The vibrating waves of exquisitely pure, translucent Light of Daniel's presence touched my heart with their secrets.

"I AM the spiraling breath of spirit, a pulsing stream of Light flowing within the tides and currents of the electrified field of Universal Consciousness. No longer caged within the limitations of my mind and its emotions, my sails are the wings of my spirit's Light, flowing through the creative matrix of spacetime that is within and without me. Keep surrendering the stagnated breath of your mind's false power to create space within your biology for the vastness of your spirit's Light to breathe through you and *as* You. Do not fear who you are becoming."

"Ellen, please drink the water I gave you to keep your connection with your body."

I slowly recognized Daniel's voice and did as he asked. Feeling more oriented, I told him there was no need to stay. After he left, I fell into a deep sleep until Angie came for her evening visit. I remembered she had offered to give me a massage and was glad to see her. Once I relaxed into the massage, a memory of myself as a teen, fighting with my mother, came to me. I was doing my best to hurt her with my impetuous comments. My mother's dark eyes showed no reaction, and her face remained calm, unmoved by my insults. In my desire to hurt her, my remarks became more caustic, and she walked away, unmoved. I began to cry. Angie said nothing but asked me to turn over to massage my chest area, and my sobs became a flood. When finished, she gave me a glass of water.

"I was a vicious monster with my mother. The ways of my parents shamed me, as my friends often commented on how odd they were, and I wanted their acceptance. While I insulted my father on occasion, my mother took the brunt of my insults, and I always attacked her when my father wasn't around. My anger burned even hotter when I saw she wouldn't allow my insults to hurt her. I knew she never told my father about my behavior because he would have told me not to treat her like that. I didn't deserve her kindness."

"Rose understood your anger and pain, but it wasn't a 'fixable' problem. You know that neither of you could change to be what the other wanted, and your growing ego wanted acceptance in the eyes of others to feel worthy and important. Even adults crave recognition from others. Your efforts to demean her did not supersede or influence who your mother knew herself to be, just as you are letting go of the need to gain acceptance from others to feel worthy. Your mother had surrendered the false power of her mind to realize the exalted wholeness of her Beingness. The Love and Light that she and your father had integrated transcended their biological relationship with you. Once you matured, they released you to experience life as you needed to, without judgment. The magic of your spirited imagination lives on in your drawings, but you had to make the choice to awaken what had died within you. I believe they have always known the courageous choice that you have made."

A week had passed since last seeing Daniel, but he stopped by today. There were few exceptions in my diet now, and he picked up deli sandwiches on his way. We had almost finished eating when he asked if I would like to hear how he met my parents. I smiled, and he began.

"Two years before Ken and Rose began taking sailing lessons from me, I took my three-year-old son sailing. The wind was perfect for sailing, but my wife did not want me to take him because it was a cool day. I ignored her wish, and she stayed home. When we were far out onto the lake, the wind changed suddenly, and I had to give my full attention to the sails to keep the boat from tipping over. I put Dean in a safe place. Trusting he would remain in his seat; I turned my back to him while adjusting the sails. A minute or so later, I heard his body fall into the lake. I quickly jumped in to get him, but the shifting wind blew in cold air, and I had few dry clothes to cover him. A week later, he was dangerously ill with pneumonia, and the doctors hospitalized him. He didn't die, but his lungs were damaged.

"My wife did not know she was a month pregnant at the time. Her difficult pregnancy and trauma of Dean's damaged lungs proved too much for her to cope with. After Mary, my daughter, was born, my wife went into a deep depression that needed treatment, and her resentment toward me only deepened her depression. She and the kids went to live with her parents. I wanted to keep the kids, but they were better off with their grandparents for many reasons, including a huge commotion had I insisted they stay with me. Soon a divorce was in the works.

"You can imagine my disheveled state when I met your parents. I did my best to present myself as together and in control when I worked with others, and most were clueless about my despair. But Ken and Rose saw right through me. They didn't ask any questions or make comments about my mental state, but I sensed their compassionate acceptance for all that was creating my pain. Their acceptance made me acutely aware of the harshness I held toward myself."

Daniel stopped to finish the rest of his sandwich. I had been listening closely and realized that my parents' eyes had always touched me with the same compassion. The brick wall of my anger blocked even a trickle of their Love and wisdom from penetrating my hardened awareness. My organized, controlling ways kept anything that could ruffle the comfortable routines of my life from surfacing. I was a psychiatrist, but my inflexible, opinionated eyes could not see the glaring billboard of my misguided ways that my awakening eyes were beginning to see. I was glad to hear Daniel continue his story.

"That day, the wind was perfect for sailing. But soon, everything changed, just like when Dean had fallen into the water. I froze, and your father suggested I sit for a moment to gather my wits. When I looked into his eyes, I saw the wind swirling within them, which somehow lifted me from my heavy despair. I swear to this day that his eyes spoke to me. 'You cannot control the bountiful grace that is of the wind. You can only understand the wind and learn to flow in harmony with it. Let go of the judgmental thoughts that rule you while filling your cells with toxins. Surrender the decay of your shallow breath to the dynamic, inner wind of your spirit's creative passion where judgment does not exist. Breathe the fullness of your spirit's Light through every fiber of your Beingness.'

"I closed my eyes and breathed the impassioned flow of the winds, swirling in opposite directions, deep within. My chest expanded, and I began to feel much lighter, as if the winds were lifting me into the open space of the sky. My anguish showed itself, but instead of pushing it deeper within to avoid feeling its pain, I allowed it to be fully present. The heavy, knotted chains that had caged my heart were releasing their density, and I kept breathing ever more deeply to free myself of my guilt-ridden pain. I experienced a melding of my presence with the swirling winds, as if I were the winds, and I knew immense joy.

"I have no idea how much time passed before opening my eyes. Your parents were trying to adjust the sails. While they lacked the skills to effectively negotiate the mechanics of the sails, I was awestruck by their intuitive sense of the direction that the wind was changing in. I knew they understood the wind's changing direction because they were of the wind. We said little as we sailed back into the harbor. I wasn't sure who, or what, had spoken to me, but I knew my experience was real. The sailing lessons continued, and more mystical experiences followed. We all knew what was going on, but we chose not to say anything. We shared a beauty that was too sacred to speak about. Those outings on the lake changed everything about me."

I nodded, knowing what he had experienced. It was the same magic that was weaving itself back into my own life. "How are Dean and Mary doing today?"

"Dean is still an asthmatic, but with the medicines available today, asthma no longer hampers him to the degree it did when he was a child. He has grown to love sailing, and we often share a day together on the lake. We've talked about the accident, and he holds no animosity toward me about it. He and Mary are in college now and have their own lives. Mary was an infant when the divorce happened, so she didn't experience the trauma of having a parent no longer with her. Life without a father in the house was normal. I spent much time with them when they were kids, and we shared memorable experiences together. But I am their father, and I know they have their gripes about me. Someday, they may choose to investigate the roots of their gripes to release them. It's their choice to make."

"And your wife?"

"She stayed with her parents for about five years while going to college to get a nursing degree. She began to date someone about three years after we separated, and once she had a job and her own place, she married him. She seems content with him and her life. We're cordial to each other. We recognize that we have gone down drastically different paths. Dean's accident was a catalyst that ignited necessary change into motion."

Daniel said he had an appointment to get to and was on his way. I had been spending more time in the library and was now reading the poems myself, although I enjoyed them more when Angie recited them. She embodied the essence the poetry held, and her voice touched me in a way that opened my breath to the majesty of the energies that the words held. But there were times when a poem called to me, and I did not want to wait for Angie. I randomly took a book from the shelf that was calling to me, and a poem about Uranus and Saturn was on the page the book opened to.

Uranus and Saturn:
Harmonized Opposites Energizing and
Imagining the Universe into Being

Uranus

My raw, primal flame burns with passion
  to create through My Light.
My passion sparks the power of attraction
  between My core of passion
  and primal Heart's core of Love.
My fiery flame hears the call of primal Water to enter Her.
Moving through Love and for Love,
  I unite with Her, inseminating Her cosmic womb
  with My fiery life force.

Saturn

My Heart, the creative force of Love,
  receives Spirit's passionate flame.
My tempering water transforms Its flame
  into the Light of all creation's potentials
  that I imagine into being.
They are the four quadrants of dimensionality—
  Divine Spirit, Divine Heart, Divine Mind, and Cosmological Life—
  as the vibrations, or principle ideas, of creation's movement.
My power of Love births Light
  into vibrating waves within form so that
  Consciousness can radiate Its beauty *as* form.

Uranus and Saturn

The intensity of our union, as passion and Love,
   creates the movement of an energy vortex
   spiraling counterclockwise and clockwise,
   inward and outward.

The emerging void of our vortex
   will fill with the multidimensionality of spacetime
   and the endless forms that I imagine into being.
And, at the Heart of the void within each being,
   beyond creation's swirling energies,
   the still, radiant Heart of sublime Love pulses.

The process of creation's energy—
   the unified, spiraling movement of
   life, death, and evolutionary expansion—has begun.
The formless becomes form,
   only to enfold inward, into its core,
   to break apart and be reborn
   as ever more exalted forms of Love and Light.

Feel the sensuous, pulsing vibration
   of your soul's loving passion.
Open to receive Its Love.
You are Love—emitting, radiating, and expanding Love.
   Realize your Immortality.

SIX

After reading the poem, I took it into the sunroom and reread it countless times. When my gaze turned to my father's painting on the floor, the reds of Pluto were pulsing with aliveness as if to call my attention to them. Their intensity grew, just as the blaze of an uncontained fire grows, and the shades of red morphed into the flames of Eliza's wavy, red hair dancing like an unrestrained wild woman. Their flames resonated with a tone of immense purity, enrapturing me with their profound passion to create, just as Eliza's singing enraptures me. Nothing could dampen the spirited fire that sang through Eliza's voice, and it was the purity of her spirit, singing through her, that drew people to her singing. She was away for two weeks to give one of her rare performances at Lincoln Center. Before she left, she said this performance would be her last opera performance.

The work of Eliza, Angie, and Daniel embodied their spirit's Light that breathed through them. I could not return to my former work and was clueless about my work down the road. But unlike the old me, I was not concerned by what I once labeled as aimlessness: being without a purpose and defined goals to reach the mountaintop. For now, I wanted to know the depth of each step that breathed through the belly of the mountain within me, where each step was the bottom, middle and top of the mountain. Within the mountain's belly was the pure, dynamic wholeness of the moment that my mind was still adjusting to and learning to dance with. Eliza's singing always transported me into the belly of my inner mountain, where my purpose was simply to exist as the inspiration that burned within it, moving only for Love and through Love.

My gaze moved to Saturn: the embodiment of the creative power of the Cosmos and my own inner, expanded Beingness. As a psychiatrist, I used the word "love" endlessly and carelessly, but I was without even an inkling of what constituted real Love. Now, I *felt* Love as an essence of exalted purity, sourced from deep within the mystical core of my Beingness. I could radiate Love and Be *as* Love, but I could not give it to another. In fact, if I believed others could harm me by denying me their love, or that I could harm others by denying them my love, then my center was the imbalanced judgment of my mind and ego. I was forever playing endless games of manipulating what I believed love to be to gain power or control over another, or of being a victim if others refused me their love. No wonder my mother could so easily remove herself from my insults. She, and my father embodied the essence of a Love deep within them that saw through the fallacy of my actions. But they also knew they would enrage me if they suggested that the love I had embraced was with limitations.

I closed my eyes and breathed out the anguish I felt for being so foolish, even though I thought of myself as being so smart and clever at that time. My auburn eyes came to my inner vision, filled with Light that spoke to me. "You recognize the fallacies of your mind because you are slowly integrating the Lightbody of your soul that illuminates what had been the darkness of your mind's ignorance. You are an original ray of the sun's radiance, but at the same time, your Lightbody shares Its center with the Original Intellect. Your radiant depths, which are of the sacred Mystery, forever renew and expand your vital life force.

"The ring around Saturn speaks to the great paradox of Love: separation is necessary for Love to experience Its own Essence. The Love of Consciousness is eternal, but Love becomes aware of Its Awareness through the human who has energetically released the patterns of love known solely through the mind and ego. Surrender the imbalanced energies of your mind's duality and allow Love to transmute these energies into droplets of wisdom that your soul absorbs within Its crystalline core. When you align your human self with your soul and spirit, universal creativity from within your timeless depths is available to create through, and you expand the creative energies of the Universe through your creations. Present through and *as* your soul's breath, you create a Love on Earth that is unique to your own Beingness.

"So you see, unification within separation forever expands the Universe and the depths of the human experience. Without this paradox of Love, the intelligent, creative powers of the Universe would be unable to expand, and the universe would collapse inward on itself. The exquisiteness of creation's endless forms would implode into the Mystery from which they arose. Although Consciousness eternally Exists, It would no longer be the Witness to ever greater reflections of Its own magnificence that creation offers, nor could It experience Its magnificence through you and *as* You. Your sense of Self is still fragile, and you are vulnerable to reestablishing old energetic patterns that knew only separation and its duality between light and dark forces that created your judgment and battles. Do not lose your attunement to your sacred core."

The play of the sun's rays woke me, inviting me to dance with the rhythmic pulse that sang within My mystical core. Imbibing the Light of the sun's rays, I stood and began to sing the scales, just as I had seen Eliza do in my vision months ago. And, like Eliza, I felt the knots about my heart increasingly loosen. Dizziness overwhelmed me, and I sat, but I did not stop singing. I sang throughout the day until Angie came at night. She had been coming every other night for a while now. The smell of the takeout in her hands helped me to regain a sense of orientation, but I used my walker to get into the kitchen, as my balance was unsteady.

"Am I correct in assuming that you've been reading one of your mother's poems?" she asked after seeing my slow, cautious walk.

"I read it last night, but if I talk about it now, I won't be able to eat this delicious food."

Angie laughed. "Good call."

After dinner, I showed her the poem I had read. "Hmm. No wonder you were a bit out in the ethers. Are you reciting the poems aloud as you read them?"

"No, I wait for you to recite them."

"It's time for you to begin to fill those words with the vibrations of your own voice and to trust that your voice is starting to speak through the clarity of your spirit's Light. Your mind is slowly accepting and embodying the intuitive knowing of your soul, and listening to your own voice reciting the poetry will help with this process."

I was not prepared for her decision, even though I knew it was best for both of us. She was a security blanket being torn from my grasping, baby hands. I protested. "But listening to you recite the poetry has been an immense help to me."

"When you broke from the structured reality you once knew, you needed my help to guide you through the process of your evolving transformation. Without your understanding of the energies that you had expanded into, your mind's fear would have arisen and taken control while sucking your awareness back into its habituated patterns of action and reaction. But you've reached the point where my help will do more harm than good. However, being that I am here right now, and you have this book with you, I'll recite one more poem."

Sun and Moon:
Sublime Consciousness Absorbing Its Experiences within Love

Sun
I AM the material Lightbody
  of Spirit's positively charged, emitting radiance
  within the electromagnetic field of Universal Awareness.
I AM Self-Aware, Self-reflective Consciousness:
  the Crystalline Core of the Universal Heart
  from which all energies flow out of and return into.

I AM the creative potential of collaboration
  among all universal forces.
The power of attraction flows into Me, and
  I bring its polarized charges into a balanced harmony
  within the movement of My spiraling vortex.

Flowing counterclockwise, the intuitive wholeness
  of the negative, feminine charge assumes order and patterns, while
Flowing clockwise, the rational order and patterns
  of the positive, masculine charge loosen and assume a wholeness.

When the dark and light sing at the same frequency
   suitable to them,
They merge into a single, pulsing point of Light
   that holds the vision of Spirit's inspiration.
As my vision lifts outward, into the Universe,
   a more expansive movement opens
   from within My depths.
Wisping wings of wisdom's Light,
   as potential holding greater interconnectedness
   with All-that-is,
Enter the depths of My expanded psyche,
   the depths of your very own psyche.

Surrender your battles between the light and the dark
   and meld your breath with My breath.
Touch the potentials of ever-expanding beauty
   within the timeless depths
   of your crystalline core.
Breathe your spirit's wisping wings of Light
   forward into time as form.

Moon
I AM the material Dark Body
   of Water's negatively charged, receiving radiance
   within the electromagnetic field of Universal Awareness.
The balanced dance between my negative charge
   and the sun's positive charge,
Forever enlivens the flow of Universal Consciousness
   as we alter and evolve the other.

My radiant darkness, deep within your own depths,
   absorbs your experiences of the
   spiritual, emotional, intellectual, and physical planes
   as pulsing droplets of wisdom that I encode and remember.

Embodying the Wisdom of Immortality

When you open to the Love of your inner, sacred Heart
  and allow Its sacred pulse
  to breathe through you and *as* You,
I digest your Heart's radiance into every fiber of your Beingness,
  enlightening You.

You are the Self-Aware Consciousness of the Divine Mind,
  absorbed within the Love of your radiant depths.
    Realize your Immortality.

The intensity of the words flowed through my lightened breath as Angie began reciting the poem. Helix shaped strands of harmoniously dancing Light came to my inner vision, singing through the immense purity of their crystalline energy. "Ellen, focus. Without focus you cannot create," the Light communicated.

I sat straight and still as I found a focus within this Light. Its intensity demanded every speck of strength I could muster. I felt lifted into an exalted realm, pulsing with sacredness, and I gave myself, completely, to this presence, just as an infant gives itself to the nurturance of the mother's breast.

"Your biology is slowly accepting the Light of your intuitive Self while allowing Its absorption into the watery depths of your DNA. The purity of Its Love and Light is transmuting your carbon-based biology into a crystalline-based biology while opening the flow of your awareness into your innermost, mystical depths. The highly subtle and dynamic nature of your core energy is intense, and it takes time to adjust to It. As your mind adjusts to the intense brilliance of your spirit's inspiration, it will get easier to keep your focus within your crystalline core. A rhythm between the wholeness of your intuitive depths and the logic of your rational mind will slowly evolve and become more natural."

Angie and I were silent for some time after she finished, each of us present within our own blissful state. At some point, her voice seamlessly entered the silence.

"There's a poem that would be helpful for you to recite in this book, and I'm going to mark the page. Give yourself time to absorb what you've heard so far before reciting it. I've never shared the story about my own inner journey, and I think it's time to do so. Like you, I was once clueless about the beauty that was within. Interested?"

I nodded.

"I need something to eat first. Would you like anything?"

"There's lots to snack on. Bring me whatever you want to have."

She disappeared into the kitchen, and I relaxed in my chair as I released some of the intensity I held. The food would help revive me a bit. I was tired, but I wanted to hear her story.

SEVEN

When the food appeared before me, my stomach growled for attention, and I happily attended to its needs. Angie was quiet as she ate, perhaps contemplating what she wanted to share.

"When your father came to the college, I had already been working there for over ten years as a chemistry professor. The excitement I once held for my work was long gone and I was experiencing burn-out. However, believing that my tenure was my ticket to a financially safe and comfortable life, I stayed. Few adults who I knew at that time, tenured or not, held the enthusiasm for their work that they had once known. Like me, they stayed with the known because there were far too many risks they had to take and sacrifices they had to make to explore a different type of work.

"The faculty was aware of the accommodations the administrators made to have your father's name associated with the college, and we were resentful of his light workload. Your father served on one committee each year, while the rest of us had a handful of committees for which we were responsible. I happened to be on the one committee he was on. Fresh eyes readily saw problems that weary eyes refused to see, and your father mentioned problems that most committee members were aware of but did not want to hear about. While his ideas for change had merit, they would have taken much time and effort to implement. So, most of us chose to believe that things were fine, just as they were, and there was no need to fix what did not need fixing.

"In addition to the heavy committee load the rest of us had, we had four courses to teach every semester versus the two courses your father had, which were both an Independent Study. They were electives, free of state curriculum standards, and your father took full advantage of the opportunity to challenge students' thinking. I was a bit aware that my resentments prevented me from acknowledging the value of his courses, but that didn't stop my anger from festering. My personal life was no better. Both my kids were away at college, and my husband and I spent our newly found free time battling our built-up resentments. I was a walking dead woman, stuck in weary, habituated patterns of daily routines, and my mind dismissed any creative flares of imagination that may tempt it to awaken from its slumber. The growing strength of my resentments was the only thing that made me feel alive.

"One day, after a vicious fight with my husband, I lit into your father about all the work the rest of us had, and our lack of time to put his suggestions into action. Most committee members didn't hesitate to join my complaints. Your father said he was unaware that his suggestions were creating hardships. Our meeting was toward the end of the spring semester, and we had only one more scheduled. At that last meeting, your father said he had spoken to the administration about a committee change, and it was in process. We knew none of us would have to deal with him again.

"Over the summer, my husband and I filed for a divorce, and I put myself in therapy in hopes that it would lift me from my growing misery. For the first time ever, I began to look at my unacknowledged anger. It was a lot to face. Shortly before the fall semester began, I saw your parents at a local event and apologized to your father. His eyes appeared to soften as if to acknowledge my pain that created the scene. Feeling a bit shaken, I quickly left the space. Being that we were both in the science department, we ran into each other now and then, and we began to chat more. The arrogant snob I believed your father to be didn't exist; I was the arrogant snob. I met Ken and Rose for dinner one night, and Rose told me about her poetry while inviting me to stop by to read it if I cared to. I didn't like poetry at that time, but for some reason, I wanted to look at her books. Unconsciously, I had stirred disaster in my life because I was ready for a major change, and your parents magically fell into my life to help bring it about.

"After that school year ended, I took what I thought would be a one-year sabbatical. I was experiencing disorientation between what I understood life to be and how your mother's poetry spoke of life. To traverse deeper into my depths to confirm what I was beginning to intuitively feel to be Truth, I had to temporarily let go of the building blocks of the science I knew and taught. I never returned."

She stopped to drink some water. "I'd like to continue, but I want to be sure it's not a problem to talk about the roadblocks I hit in traditional therapy. Do you mind?"

"No, go on. It's likely that I would say the same thing about my former work."

She nodded, then continued. "After a couple of years reading your mother's poetry and talking to your parents about it, I left therapy. I was getting stuck in the processing of my life experiences while blaming others for my pain and suffering, even though I understood they had suffered, too, and their actions were based on what they could understand about life. I hit a brick wall, and your mother's poetry became my tool to help dissolve it. I began to get massages to help move tension out of my body, and it dawned on me that I would be a good massage therapist. So, I pursued that line of work. What I would have negated as complete nonsense before I got to know your parents has become my inner, guiding light.

"When I met your parents, I felt very lost, and I had to face endless discomfort, even anguish, about who I had been and what motivated my actions. I also went through periods of doubt where I went into a panic about leaving my profession and making a fool out of myself by believing that the energy I was experiencing was real. How talented the mind is to seed doubt, repeatedly and forcefully, to protect its own life force. Yet, I knew it was too late for me to turn back, as I had experienced too much Love to negate Its beauty. Those were challenging times. Slowly, surely, my mind dropped its battles with my intuitive Self as the years passed. It now understands that it has no need to judge my past behavior: it was simply a reflection of lacking alignment with the radiance of my sacred center. Most times, when my awareness slips into Earth's density, such that my mind starts to take control, I'm able to get myself out of it before I lose my way in it."

She sighed and said goodnight.

"Good night, Angie. And I'm not at all surprised by the roadblocks you hit with your therapist. Like you, I can now admit what I had refused to acknowledge not so long ago."

The dazzling luster of the autumn colors was fading, and the leaves were falling to nourish earth's soil as I drove to the harbor for a day of sailing with Daniel and others he invited, including Angie and Eliza. Hints of winter's frigid, howling wind were beginning to tease us, and his boat would soon find its covered place of winter slumber. I never cared much for the winter, but this year, I was looking forward to seeing the land blanketed in snow and feeling the strength of the wind against my body. As soon as Daniel disengaged the boat from the dock, the wind filled its sails. As we sailed out of the harbor, I embraced the wind, inviting its wild, spirited dance to help me release my oncoming anxiety related to my office. It had been eight months since my life-changing event, and I decided to close my office permanently. Doubt about my future was drumming its death march of doom, loud and clear. I had yet to recite the poem that Angie had marked for me, as my growing doubt about the future distracted me from gaining the clarity necessary to feel the poem's essence sing through me.

While we all welcomed the sounds of the unrestrained wind moving the sails and touching our bodies as it swirled about us, its roar made it difficult to hear people talk. Its strength teased my sense of balance, and my hand clenched a support bar. Remembering that balance was within, not without, I loosened my grip just a bit. I assured myself that I can adjust to the ongoing changes ahead while also keeping my sense of inner balance and harmony.

Eliza's quiet was a stranger to me. The rays of the bright sun danced as tempered flames of wisdom through Eliza's wavy red hair. I sensed discernment in those flames; they would burn only what needed purification and do no harm. Eliza's sky-blue eyes turned toward me, inviting me to see the secrets held within them. I breathed the robustness of the wind through me and met her piercing gaze with my eyes. The intensity filling her gaze jolted me, and I closed my eyes. Within my inner vision, my naked body appeared, filled with swirling winds of Light, blowing in all directions, which were loosening the constraining knots of my oncoming anxiety.

"You are a seeker of Truth," the winds whispered through my breath. "The foundations of the structures you have so steadfastly built and sustained are collapsing as they need to. Face your fear of change, fully, and breathe the fullness of your inner wisdom through you. Allow the discernment of your soul's wisdom to blow away the foundations of your false, conditioned truths while unveiling Truth within. Be present within your center, balanced in spirit, heart, mind, and body as you move through your mind's perceived obstacles. These obstacles are merely energies that are trying to pull your awareness out of your core center of Love and into your ego center of fear, where they can assert power and control.

"In making the choice to release the tense, confining movement of your decayed beliefs and structures, you open space within you to enable the subtle, highly dynamic essence of Love to breathe through you. The wisdom of spirit recognizes that one must continuously shed the old into the void of the swirling vortex, just as a serpent sheds its skin. Within its still depths, Love renews the ashes of what has been into forms of ever expanded beauty. To be rooted within your still center of Love, is to be rooted within a presence of balanced harmony, regardless of ongoing changes about your center."

I released my doubt to the rotating winds, moving clockwise and counterclockwise. While traces remained that would tease me, my doubt lost the intense force of its false power that was looking to control my choices. I was beginning to recognize the difference between wisdom's discernment and my mind's nonstop thoughts and judgments as my inner and outer worlds came together into a unified, harmonized dance. I could, and I would, move through the process of permanently closing my office through grace.

Today matched the beauty of yesterday, and I went outside without my walker. I seldom used it while walking around the house, but I always took it with me when I went outside, just to be on the safe side. Today, however, I freed myself from its support. Letting go of my dependence on the walker was a symbolic gesture of freeing myself from the support systems that had once defined me when I had not aligned my human heart with my mystical Heart. It was time to read the poem Angie had marked for me, and I took it outside with me. Breathing the wind deep within, I began to read.

Jupiter and Mars: Building Up and Breaking Down

Jupiter

I AM the receptive container of cosmological creativity
   receiving the Light of Consciousness into My bosom.
I stabilize and help sustain Its brilliance
   by intuiting Its inner design and organizing It
   into patterns and systems, energetically and materially.

You become attached to your creations and enamored
   with your stabilizing sense of individuality.
Fear of the unknown
   insidiously appears and grows.
You build protective walls around you and your creations.
Your mind's stagnating breath of decay
   veils your spirit's breath of Light
   that once flowed fluidly within you.

A deep sense of incompleteness
   gnaws from within.
You grow tired of your ceaseless striving, and
   you question the habituated patterns of your existence.
Out of Love and through Love,
   release your cage of stagnation and decay.

Mars

I AM Spirit's fiery passion:
  the life force that sparked all existence into being.
I burn the decay of life and reform its ashes
  into ever more vibrant forms of radiance.

Through Love,
  meet the dragons of your dark shadow.
Break through the fear of your dragon's fiery breath, and
  Light will illumine your darkness
  with Its Love and wisdom.
Perceive Truth and Love
  beyond the veil of your ignorance.
Serve the passion of your spirit's life force.

You can choose to rebuild the new
  through the limited, imbalanced center
  of your mind's restrictive breath.
A breath solely of linear time,
  devoid of the subtle Love that renews life.
          or
You can choose to rebuild the new
  through the unlimited, balanced center
  of Love's free-flowing grace.
A Breath that originates from the timeless order
  of your radiant, dark depths,
 Flows into the time order of the Earth realm
  where your mind gives order and design to Its brilliance,
And returns into your core to renew your life force
  as an ever-expanding Breath of creative vision.
    The choice is yours.

I recited the poem slowly. I *felt* the brilliance of its vibrations flow through me as my own breath merged with its purity. Angie was right. I had reached a point where it was important for my mind and body to experience the vibrations of my changing voice. Each time I recited the poem, my voice expanded into the fullness of the presence that the words embodied. Increasingly, my mind's resistant growls were becoming soft purrs of acceptance.

EIGHT

E ach day I took care of another detail to put closure on the decayed and dying chapter of the person I once was and the life I had created. Feeling a bit overwhelmed, I called Jean, hoping she had time to help with the details of ending a career she had so diligently supported. Unlike the last time I spoke to her, she was not surprised by my choice. When she shared her news that she was pregnant and had not looked for another job, I understood why she showed no surprise. She had reacquainted herself with her long-lost passion for cooking and was enjoying life more than she could ever have imagined. Fortunately, her body was handling the pregnancy well, and she had the strength and time to help close the office.

I had a condominium in the city, and I called a realtor about putting it up for sale. She agreed to look at it and get back to me about what I needed to do before putting it on the market. I had lived there for years and knew people to contact to get the place ready once I heard from the realtor. Each day, I called a colleague to put closure on anything left unresolved by my sudden departure. I had often met many of them for dinner, but none would be able to understand the person I was becoming. If I tried to explain myself, they would judge me, just as I had once judged my parents. It was best to keep things on the surface.

My brief talks with them made me aware of the vastly different centers we existed within and who I once was. I had been completely unaware of my deeper Truth, but I understood how it was possible for me to be so ignorant of It. I felt, and I saw the heaviness of gravity that bonded society's truths together. These tightly assembled energies lived inside people as inflexible thought patterns and emotions that few saw a need to question. Angie once shared that when my father began his career, he was climbing the academic mountain outside of him. At that time, he believed his research would unveil the deep mysteries of the Universe. But when he saw cracks in the foundational truths that supported his research, he stopped and dealt with them. He hit a wall where he could no longer function in the science in which he had lost faith. He intuitively gleaned his understanding, and the means to "prove" his work did not exist within objective science. In fact, his colleagues would have dismissed him if he expressed his truth, just as I once did.

My father used his independent study courses at the small college to guide students in the "art" of questioning while revealing the cracks in the foundations of their beliefs. What his students chose to do, once those cracks surfaced, was their choice. The great majority chose to cover the cracks and move on with who they knew themselves and the world they created to be. To acknowledge those cracks was to invite drastic change into the foundation of every aspect of their existence. I now understood the sacrifices my parents made, but I also understood they had become rich in ways that society could not see or understand. However, my father was careful by keeping his artwork in the poetry books anonymous, as well as his help in writing them so that other scholars would not question him. He did not want to lose the opportunity to work with students.

If my own break from the tightly ordered reality I had known was not so sudden and drastic, I, too, would have continued to ignore the cracks closing in on me. There were far too many risks to my ego's security and my mind's attachments to all it had identified with to deal with disruptive inconsistencies. My anger toward my parents, especially my mother, was a shield my mind had created to prevent me from perceiving what it could not understand. It would do anything necessary to protect itself, including ramping up the force of its emotions, like anger, to veil what it perceived as a threat to its power. Light did not force Its presence upon anyone. I had to be open to feel and receive Its radiance and breathe Its purity through me. My state of shock from my parents' sudden death lowered my mind's resistance, creating the conditions for my intense breakthrough.

Eliza stopped in for a visit today and told me about her new project. Having freed herself of her demanding and restrictive schedule, she was extending her roots and branches into unknown territory. During one of her trips, about a year ago, she connected with a songwriter who had been in the music business even longer than her.

"Carol is not a well-known artist, but her guitar and voice sing through the presence of Light's clarity, and I knew my voice could easily blend with hers when I heard her sing. Most of her music was country rock, and she grew tired of the human tales of love and woe in her songs. She wanted to create songs that transcended human drama and to expand the genre of music she had given most of her attention to. Our music is a blend of styles unique to our experiences. We've been doing most of our work online, with Carol playing her guitar, but we're getting to the point where I'll have to go to New York City on occasion to be with an orchestra

Carol enjoys working with to record our music. I've listened to her sing and play her guitar with the orchestra, and I like its sound."

I congratulated her. The seeds to Eliza's new venture were well-rooted and beginning to sprout their magnificence. While I knew seeds were gestating within me that had yet to bud into form, I was still without a conscious, focused direction. The seeds were with their own directive principle, and I had to allow the tension of their gestation before the masculine energy of rational order revealed the patterns and designs the seeds would assume materially. If I forced my human will and my mind's logic on my spirit's gestating inspiration, I would limit the beauty its form could radiate. I am learning the patience of an artist's creative spirit and growing in my ability to trust and nurture the intuitive process of my imagination's unfolding. My compass was becoming my inner, intuitive wisdom of reverence for all life, and institutions and doctrines outside of me were no longer necessary to define my beliefs and morality. Most institutions had become embedded in their own agendas of power and control, and I wanted no part of that energy.

I met Daniel at a café for lunch today. Our friendship was deepening as my sensitivity to the multidimensional space he existed within opened within me. I felt immense ease when talking to him. Acting through his inner sense of justice, his spirit's discernment kept him free. While I valued my friendship with Daniel, our chemistry did not ignite the passionate sparks between lovers. Besides, Daniel shared an intimate relationship with a woman who he had met about four years after his divorce. At that time, they both had young children and felt it best to keep their separate living space. By the time the kids were older, they had grown comfortable with their arrangement and decided to keep things as they were. While the love they shared was deep, they were both fiercely independent, and they knew it would be difficult to adjust to living together all the time.

"What I share with Jane is uniquely special, and whether we live together or not, has little to do with its beauty," Daniel said as we ate. "While we share a great amount of time together, and often stay at each other's place now that the kids no longer live at home, having our own space is a necessity. Loneliness doesn't exist for either of us, although I have found that people associate living alone with loneliness. We've both received many unpleasant comments about our choice, but we don't let them under our skin. I don't want entanglement with the judgment of any mind, including my own, should I slip into the space where judgment festers."

I nodded. "My work once filled my living space, both within and without. It was my identity. Back then, if noise didn't fill my space, I would have been lonely. Now, space from others and the chatter of my own mind is a necessity. If I met someone who sent my heart soaring, I would consider living with him, but I can't see myself getting married again. It worked for my parents, but the essence that breathed through their relationship, and that kept it so vibrantly alive, transcended the institution of marriage as society defines it. Speaking of my parents, you've never spoken about my mother's poetry. Did you ever read it?"

"The first couple of years I knew them, we met only for sailing. They never talked about their work, nor did I question them about it. Their eyes always felt to lift me into the free-flowing grace of the wind where nothing, other than sailing the boat, mattered. The wind, within and without me, was increasingly becoming my teacher. I came to understand that it was always the wind, the presence of my own spirit's Light flowing within me, that lifted me into the expanded space of my Beingness. Your parents were guides who helped to ignite my spirit's passion, although I had to sense the Light within them and allow It to touch me to open to my own inner Light."

When Daniel stopped talking, the golden threads in the sea of his turquoise eyes began to swirl, in all directions, while touching the open space within me. "You are the electrified Cosmos, the embodiment of the spiraling winds of your spirit's creative imagination. Your physical body is not the Truth of your Beingness, nor are your beliefs your Truth. Be the magician who exists as the balanced, unified flow of cosmic energy within the core of your sacred Self. Embody the dynamics of the transcended psyche. Realize your Self as an integrated whole within your crystalline core."

The harbor was close to the café, and I took advantage of my newly gained independence of driving to stop there on my way home. The cold air grounded me. As I watched winter's vigorous, swirling winds stir the water, I allowed them to stir my own inner depths while extending my roots deep into the open space of my radiant sea. I was surprised at the time that had passed as I sat by the lake and was exhausted when I got home. I made a quick dinner and yielded my body to my warm bed early. The following morning, after making coffee, I sat in the sunroom. One of my mother's poetry books was on the coffee table, and I opened it to reveal the poem I was to recite.

Venus and Mercury:
Crystalline Vision Embodied and Symbolized

Venus
I am the witness to your seeking.
Through Love,
   you have faced the depths of your darkness while
   shedding the falsehoods of your conditioned ancestry.
Now cleansed of the toxins that veiled

Embodying the Wisdom of Immortality

Love's expansive space within your depths,
You are digesting the essence of Love
  within each cell of your Beingness.

    You realize—
I AM the electromagnetic field of conscious Awareness:
  the passionate essence of My Spirit's Light
  crystallized as the creative vision of my psyche.
I AM aware of My Awareness.

Mercury

My fiery passion,
  transmuted into the Light of Imagination through Love,
  draws all opposing energies of my spiraling vortex together
  while placing a single, directive principle at My core.
Love and Light have reconciled all conflict
  between the positive male and negative female energies.
The Breath that enlivens My inward and outward life
  harmoniously flows as One unified movement
  within the vastness of My crystalline core.

    You realize—
I AM the vibratory Intelligence of My Crystalline Heart:
  an instantaneous, direct knowing
  of Love's discerning wisdom.
I *feel* the innocent radiance
  of My Heart's Love and wisdom
  echo through My sacred chambers.
Its perceptive intuition, solely, guides all actions.

Through sublime Love and Truth, and
As sublime Love and Truth,
  I infuse My radiance within cultural symbols and systems.

NINE

S unrises illuminating the darkness of night and sunsets returning the night's darkness to Earth marked the coming and passing of my days. And between the daily melding of darkness into light and light into darkness, I recited my mother's poetry. Each poem took me deeper into the exquisiteness of my own inner radiance. My inner, ethereal sea of sublime grace gave no credence to the passing of calendar days, and I paid little attention to time. The growing howls of the wind gave voice to the oncoming winter, and their slow transformation into softening currents of air gave voice to the oncoming spring. I enjoyed taking walks while experiencing the changing tones of the wind upon my skin and the serenity of the barren land as its seeds of new life gestated beneath its blanket of snow. I forever surrendered all I had once known myself to be into the crystalline core of my own inner depths. As winter's gestating seeds slowly began to reveal the buds of their future magnificence, I wondered if I, too, would begin to see the forms that the gestating seeds within me would assume.

The night sky increasingly captured my attention as winter passed. The white blanket of snow covering Earth's surface accentuated the clear, crisp vibrations the stars and planets resonated. Often, I stilled every speck of movement within me to experience the quiet pulse of the Universal Heart that cradled the stars and planets in Its unspeakable magnificence. Tonight, as I peered into the clear, night sky, I saw only the radiant darkness of the new moon. I sat to fully imbibe its exquisite beauty, and as I did so, a golden thread of Light appeared from within the moon's belly that spiraled toward me, touching me with Its presence. I lost myself to this immense, exalted Love.

"Always exist within the exalted Love of your soul and spirit that your transformed, crystalline DNA is digesting into every fiber of your Beingness. When you are fully aware *as* the free-flowing breath of your spirit's Light, your golden wings of imagination will take flight. The seeds of your creative endeavor have been rooted and ripened, and they are almost ready to reveal their form to the world. They will present themselves in their own way and in their own time. Remain present in the Love that is constant beyond the appearance of change and allow this Love to serve you. Find patience within Love's stillness where time does not exist."

I sat outside for quite some time, mesmerized by the moon's translucent beauty. The air that was growing chilly could not distract my attention from the sublime grace that consumed me. Staying balanced within all aspects of my Beingness, while serving the grace of my own soul, was a day-to-day adventure filled with trial and error. But the Love I had opened to and that now breathed through the deepest essence of my Beingness defined me, and I would do whatever was necessary to create through my spirit's inspiration. I sighed, made my way to my bed, and I soon lost myself in the dream world. It was strange how the boundary between my dream world and waking world felt far less solid.

I began most days with coffee in the sunroom, reciting a poem, while allowing its depth to breathe through me, and Daniel continued to join me at times. The beauty of my parents' souls, which the poetry resonated with, harmoniously blended with my own soul's emerging beauty within me. Its pure splendor helped my mind to serve the Light of my soul's imagination, rather than trying to control It. I wanted to breathe the Light and Love of my core Self through my entire Beingness and Be as my soul and spirit in all actions.

Today, after some shopping together, Angie and I had coffee. "I have a client, a woman, who you may want to work with. She's going through a challenging midlife crisis and is seeking a deeper meaning to her life. Have you given any attention to your future creative endeavors?"

Angie ignited the spark of passion gestating within me, and I knew I wanted to work with this woman. "It's going to be a bit of exploration as I find my way into the new form my work will assume, but I'd like to have her information to talk to her."

"I've been giving her massages for the past six months, and while I'm just beginning to know her, I recognize her spirited, intuitive nature. I'll give you her information, and you can call her when you feel ready to. But if you could reach out to her within the next couple of weeks, I'd appreciate it. She asked if I knew of anyone who could help her, and I said I knew someone who may be interested. She's waiting for me to get back."

"I'll give her a call within the next couple of weeks. I need time to get a sense of how I'll present my work to her."

Angie grinned and left. I put one of Eliza's CDs into the stereo, retrieved a notepad, and started to jot down any ideas that came to me about my new work. I was confident that my random jots would eventually define the foundational structure of it. And I would keep that structure fluid by staying attuned to the rhythmic flow of my spirit's inspiration within and acting only through It.

The rhythmic pulse of my inner Heart weaved its essence through my budding work as my inner and outer worlds melded together into a unified flow. I was learning the "art" of working with a creative tension as I gave form to My spirit's imaginative Light. It was not a fear-based tension of the unknown future. Rather, it was a tension rooted in a Love that I did not want to contaminate: the future was already present within the gestating seed of my spirit's vision, and my "work" was to nurture Its creative essence as it unfolded into time. However, traces of my mind's past tendencies, such as infusing its agendas into my work as well as its impatience to get things done, remained, and I had to be vigilant to avoid overriding the fullness of the gestating Light within me.

I decided to use the library for my workspace. My parents had worked there, and the magical Love of transformation that breathed within it would help me through the rough patches of my unfolding work. In the end, it was up to me to trust the intuition of my own soul and allow Its Love to breathe within the space of the library. Puzzling my way through things was part of the process, as the questions that arose took me ever deeper into my radiant depths of wisdom to answer them. I was setting the wings of my imagination free to soar, and my support was the completeness of who I was becoming. I just needed to trust the intuitive wisdom of my inner Self.

I asked Daniel if he would come by today to help move a couple of pieces of furniture in the library, and he appeared to absorb himself in the room's energy. "I've only been in this room once or twice, and while I felt the magic of this space, I could never fully relax in it. You know how much I disliked school and books, which included libraries. Oddly, I don't feel any of that intimidation now. I suppose I've resolved the angst of my past school years to feel the presence this space holds."

"I had avoided this space my entire adult life before my parents' passing. I disliked them for what I considered to be their weirdness, which included their work. But everything changed when I released their ashes into Lake Erie. It was a magical moment that opened me to receive the Light that vibrates within their work."

"Their spirits were present with us that day. Their Light hovered about us as we sailed out onto the lake, and I sensed their guidance in managing the speed of the boat as you released their ashes into the wind. I saw you open to feel the presence of their Light, and I wasn't surprised about the shape you were in when Angie told me. I hope you don't mind me sharing that even though you were light-years away from being in the best of shape, I was excited about the life-changing opportunity before you. And you took on the challenge with grace."

I laughed. "The purity of the Love I felt was beyond anything I had ever experienced, and there was no way I could not surrender to It. However, I'm extremely glad I didn't know what was ahead because fear would have gotten in the way of my transformation."

He smiled and was quiet for some time as if to be thinking about something. "Your parents' accident and death has perplexed me. They were the best sailors I knew, even better than myself. They could readily intuit the changing movements of the winds and knew how to get out of harm's way. I'm coming to believe they called the turbulent winds to them, to help lift them from their bodies."

I recalled Angie telling me she was not surprised at my parents' death as they had been talking about leaving their bodies behind. At that time, I was in shock about their passing, and I had completely forgotten her words. When I shared Angie's words with Daniel, he nodded. I was surprised to see him wander to the shelves holding poetry books about the planets. I did not realize that on the cover of a book was a painting of the Earth I had made years ago, and when Daniel showed it to me, I gasped.

"I'm always amazed at the clarity of my paintings. Although they are of a child, they show the energies of the planets I felt singing through them when I looked through my father's telescope. And reconnecting to those energies, as an adult, has enabled me to root them within my deepest depths."

Daniel took the book into the sunroom, and I followed him. He did the same thing I always did, allowing the book's energies to select a poem for him.

Earth: The Completeness of Radiating Beauty

You have integrated and rooted the Love and wisdom
  of Cosmic Fire, Cosmic Water, Cosmic Wind, and Cosmic Earth—
  the Divine Children of Earth's cosmic womb—
  within the womb of your very own purified psyche.

    You realize—
I AM the free-flowing stream
  of My spirit's visionary Light
Within the unified realms of
  the conscious and unconscious,
  the manifest and unmanifest,
  the self and "That" which transcends the self,
Radiating my crystallized vision on Earth.

Having released my spirit's vision into the Universe,
I surrender all that I know Myself to be
  into the deeper movement that has opened
  within the infinite depths of My inner, ethereal sea.
The spiral of life, death, and evolutionary expansion
  begins a new cycle.

Light and dark, birth and death:
They are the cyclic tides and currents of my winds
   as they spiral, in all directions,
   about My still depths of transformative Love.

As the creator and the created,
I forever expand deeper
   into the Love and Truth of Self, and
   into the experience of Self,
Through My creations and *as* My creations.

    The songs of the arriving birds welcoming spring joined Daniel as he recited the poem, and we laughed when he finished. His playful eyes met mine, and we hurried outside to breathe the fullness of the budding spring into us. We laid on the warming ground and became silent. Tiger eyes showed themselves behind my closed eyes; they were the eyes of my soul speaking directly into my Heart.

    "You have integrated the subtle, creative energies of the Cosmos within the core of your Beingness, and My spirited imagination now flows freely through you and *as* You. Stay focused within the completeness of My creative breath, which is now your very own creative breath. Do not yield to the tension of your rational mind that may want to override the rhythm of My unfoldment into form. The time and the timeless orders, the intuitive and the rational knowing, and the inner and the outer worlds come together as One integrated vision in their own way and at their own pace. Allow space for exploration and revisions in your work and remain true to the creative process, regardless of the challenges ahead. Growth can only reveal itself through change. There's no such thing as failure."

    "Would you mind if I took the book home for a week or so?" Daniel asked. "The poem is beating through me, and I'd like more time with it."

As I focused my awareness back on the beauty of the spring day, I saw Daniel getting ready to leave, and I nodded my consent. I stayed outside for quite some time, attentive to the awakening sounds of spring. I lost myself in my soul's presence. It was enjoying Its newly found experience of witnessing, through my eyes, the renewal of Its shared life force with the endless forms that nature was now birthing into being.

TEN

The textures and tones in my work with Lily, my new client, slowly revealed themselves. Lily came to me because she felt blocked by the patterns and designs of her artwork, and I knew she was seeking inspiration beyond the borders of her mind and the beliefs and emotions contained within those borders. Contrary to my former work, I gave minimal attention to the mental analysis of specific life experiences. Focusing on them, as I once did, only reinforced her mind's powerful emotions that had infused themselves into her life experiences while strengthening her attachment to energies that veiled the creativity of her inner depths. The techniques I once used were bandages over wounds "healed" at the superficial level of the mind and ego, and they always resurfaced over time.

I was learning to guide Lily in opening to and *feeling* the pure, pulsing wisdom within her crystalline core. The Light of her spirit was fluid and flowing, moving only through mystical Love. Expanding her breath beyond her mind's fear-based actions and reactions and into the pure, multidimensional space of her core, free of all of society's structures and ideations, would take time. It had taken years of inner work for Angie, Eliza, and Daniel to come into the wisdom they now embodied, and I knew that the extreme nature of my situation was a rare exception to the time necessary for most. Each person would have their own rhythm, and I had to be sensitive to, and work with that rhythm. If I pushed too much, too soon, the mind's fear could become so forceful that it would lose its gradual opening to an essence that was far more dynamic and brilliant than with what it was familiar.

My inner changes reflected the outer changes in my life. To my great surprise, I was enjoying the space of my childhood home more each day, and I was making it into the home of my changing adult self. Like my inner home, I was letting go of the old to create space for the new, but I changed little in the library and the sunroom. I sometimes laughed at the possibility that my parents knew all along I would be using this space for my work, and they designed the library for my work in the latter years of their life. Frequently, my mother's poetry sang its songs of wisdom to Lily as I recited it. I also used music in my work, and Eliza's CDs were front and center. She and Carol planned to release their first CD soon, and I was looking forward to adding it to my collection.

Angie recently referred a couple of new clients to me. She knew when people were ready for my work, and I was happy to accept them. Angie was my main guide through my own transformation. I was in an extremely fragile state when she found me. I shuddered to think of what could have happened to me if someone else, other than Eliza and Daniel, found me in the state I was in. That person would have taken me to the hospital, and the doctors would have placed me in the care of a traditional psychiatrist, which was not what my situation called for. Had that happened, I never would have come into the integrated wholeness that now defines my Beingness. In fact, I would not even be aware that my human identity was only a small aspect of my wholeness. No wonder I was feeling so much discontent at the time of my parents' passing.

Angie was the expert in the work I was taking on, and I once questioned why she referred people to me when she was fully capable of working with them. She said the work was not within her comfort zone, and she kept her boundaries with others. Angie helped because she knew no one else who could help me. She did what she knew she had to do, acting through the compassion of her soul. While I continued to seek her guidance at times, she seldom gave me answers. Instead, she asked questions that guided me to act through my own wisdom. "You can now sense the wisdom of your own soul, absorbed through the purification of your experiences, and your spirit's inspiration flowing within you. I understand you are stepping into unfamiliar territory with your work, and while I'm happy to act as a sounding board, you need to trust your own inner guidance," Angie had said to me. And I did not challenge her wishes because I fully understood them.

My improved health made it possible for me to explore the area, and I continued to enjoy sitting on a bench overlooking Lake Erie. On occasion, Daniel invited me and a few others for a day of sailing, and my love for sailing grew. Jane, his partner, was usually with us. Although quiet, her eyes revealed her wild, untamed nature that blended with the wind. After meeting Jane, I understood why she and Daniel had their own living space: the wind required lots of open space to breathe its Light within. It loses its essence, the majesty of its Light, when it feels confined. No wonder they both loved sailing.

I am alone in the sunroom this evening as the orange-red rays of the dimming sun meld with the golden yellow painting of the sun on the floor. The intense beauty of the blended colors radiating from the sun takes my breath away, and I close my eyes to experience its fullness. The tiger's eyes, infused with this radiating Light, are present, and they invite me to blend with their presence. My physical body is a still statue as I digest every speck of Light's exquisiteness within my porous cells. Golden wisps of Light arise from within the depths of my sacred, inner well while assuming the shape of wings: the golden wings of my spirit, the Holy Grail of Immortality, were before me.

I breathe into the depthless space of my core Beingness. Merging the totality of my breath with my spirit's free-flowing spiraling breath of Light, my wings of Light take flight. My sublime presence expands into the sunroom and beyond. I am a tree in full bloom, rooted in the unified, spiraling flow of energies between Earth and Heaven and enveloped in the Love that is beyond all creation, but which illuminates all creation. My cage dissipates into the black hole of my sacred center, and I am free. With or without a body, I Exist.

Acknowledgments

The work of countless mystics and innovative scholars has influenced how I have come to know Truth, although the work of those listed below has had the greatest impact on this specific book. However, my own intuitive sensitivity, which has evolved over years of inner work, has shaped the teachings of others into my own unique perspective. As such, this book is not a direct representation of the work of any one scholar or mystic. Their teachings were guides on my path that helped me open to the clarity of my own Truth, and I am grateful their work came to me.

David Bohm
Pamela Eakins
Geoffrey Hoppe: Receptive channel for Tobias and Adamus Saint-Germain
Humberto Maturana
Ira Progoff
Joseph Rael

About the Author

BETSEY GROBECKER received a doctorate in Learning, Cognition and Development and pursued an academic career believing it would help her to better understand intelligence. Disillusioned with the science of her discipline, she left everything behind to uncover the mysteries of inner wisdom. She has worked with spiritual masters of various traditions from around the world. This story reflects the wisdom gleaned from all her life experiences, including her own journey into her intuitive depths.

Other Books by Betsey Grobecker

Serpent Vision: Science, Metaphor, Story

The Lotus of the Dragon

Imagination: Passion Meeting Love

The Inner Well and Ayahuasca

Justice Beyond Duality

www.ingramcontent.com/pod-product-compliance
Lightning Source LLC
LaVergne TN
LVHW041234080426
835508LV00011B/1198